CW00959240

Crucial Skills

an Anger Management and Problem Solving Teaching Programme for High School Students

by

Penny Johnson

and

Tina Rae

a Rae

I

ISBN: 1 873 942 67 2

Lucky Duck Publishing Ltd
3 Thorndale Mews, Clifton, Bristol, BS8 2HX
Tel: 0117 973 2881 Fax: 0117 973 1707
email: publishing@luckyduck.co.uk

Printed in England by The Book Factory, 1a Mildmay Avenue, London, N1 4RS

website: www.luckyduck.co.uk

Contents

Introduction and Background

This programme is designed to be used in the secondary phase and is aimed at students who experience difficulties in managing their behaviour within a range of school contexts. It aims to empower students to manage their behaviour and feelings positively, and enable them to avoid situations of conflict. It promotes the belief that students can effect change and that it is possible to resolve difficulties and achieve a positive outcome.

Recent research has highlighted concerns about student disaffection and disruptive behaviour and the effects these might have on teaching and learning and, indeed the wider cost to society. Disaffection amongst students often leads to disruptive behaviour, truancy and in some cases permanent exclusion from mainstream schooling. Recent government documentation states:

> "that children who become disaffected fail to gain the educational and social skills they need to succeed in adult life, while at the same time using up a disproportionate share of the resources available to educate all children." (DfEE, 99)

The government has committed itself to providing funding to reduce truancy and exclusions by one third by the year 2002 and to ensure that all students excluded from school for more than 15 days receive full-time and appropriate education. Such an initiative will require LEAs and schools to re-evaluate their systems and ensure that strategies are in place for addressing student disaffection and disruptive behaviour. All LEAs are now required to have a Behaviour Support Plan in place which requires them to set out arrangements for educating students with behavioural difficulties and the roles of other relevant parties. Mainstream schools will be responsible for the education of the majority of students with behaviour difficulties, including the management of behaviour and identification of the causes of the problems. It is anticipated that schools will develop a preventative approach to managing behaviour difficulties by early identification and the implementation of support at an early stage.

It is consequently important that LEAs and schools are aware of students who are at risk of exclusion and that they adopt preventative approaches to working with such groups of students. Concerns about under-achievement are topical, and in particular concerns about the under achievement of boys. It is no coincidence that nationally boys are three times more likely to be permanently excluded than girls. (Hinds, 98)

A Preventative Approach

This programme aims to provide teachers with a preventative approach to enable students to develop the skills they need. It is aimed at those students who are experiencing difficulty in managing anger and areas of conflict. It is envisaged that the school will have already worked on such difficulties with the students and that the school's SEN and pastoral systems will have worked closely together. This work may have involved parental involvement, systems for monitoring student progress, mentoring schemes, individual behaviour plans and outside agency involvement. Typically students would have been identified and placed at stages 2 or 3 of the Code of Practice. The focus is on helping students to identify and recognise the triggers to anger and conflict and then support them in developing strategies to manage this conflict and the types of problems that they may regularly be experiencing in the school context. The course is designed to be used with a group of between 6-10 students.

Objectives

This series of lessons has been designed to meet the following objectives:

- To enable/encourage students to become reflective regarding their own behaviour and the consequences of that behaviour.
- To encourage students to develop self help strategies in order to manage and control anger and strong feelings.
- To encourage students to identify situations which may lead to conflict.
- To raise self-esteem and consequently the locus of control enable students to further develop and appreciate the perspectives of others i.e. develop empathy.
- To develop staff awareness of a range of strategies to manage challenging behaviour.
- To raise staff awareness of the possibility of developing their own skills in managing conflict situations in the classroom context.
- To raise staff awareness as to how they can differentiate the curriculum and of behaviour management strategies so as to ensure inclusion.
- To enable the whole school staff to review current school practice and to develop initiatives to promote inclusive practice particularly for students at risk.

Basic Structure of the Programme

Session 1   One to one sessions with students who will be included in the programme.

Session 2   Completion of crucial skills questionnaire and development of individual student profile.

Session 3   Brainstorming to identify triggers to anger. Setting group circle rules and articulating needs.

Session 4   Teachers use situation cards identifying triggers to anger and model alternative responses.
Use of video to record scenes.

Session 5   Students use situation cards reflecting triggers to anger. Students role play.
Use of video to record scenes.

Session 6   Viewing of role play session and use of tick box review form to identify differences between first and second scene i.e. identify strategies. Students then identify personal strategies.

Session 7   Discussion of anger management strategies. Students to feedback personal strategies. Introduction of a range of anger management ideas. Use of problem pages.
In pairs identify solutions and feedback to the group.

Session 8   Role play. Students model appropriate responses in a range of situations. Use of new situation cards and encouragement of students to use new and further developed strategies.
Use of video to record these scenes.

Session 9   View the video/role play and identify the skills they are using.
Case history of year 8 student.
Students draw up an action plan for this student.

Session 10 Evaluation of programme and looking forward.
Developing new targets.
My Action Plan.

IEPs

This programme can form the basis of a whole school preventative approach towards anger and conflict management. It aims to promote positive behaviour and believes that through effective support which uses a range of strategies within a clear system and structure, students will begin to manage their anger more successfully and avoid conflict. This work may form part of a whole school approach to training staff to respond appropriately to students who are experiencing emotional and behavioural difficulties. It provides opportunities to share good practice with teachers. The ongoing work within the group can inform target-setting as part of individual education plans (IEPs) or individual behaviour plans (IBPs).

Mentoring Scheme and Partnership with Parents/Carers

It may be considered appropriate to implement a mentoring scheme which will run alongside the crucial skills course. This allows the students to work with a trusted adult and the focus can be on target-setting, reviewing progress and further discussion of successful strategies for further managing behaviour. The mentor should be regularly updated on the ongoing work within the Crucial Skills Course. Once the course has ended the continuation of the mentoring scheme will ensure support is still in place for the student. The mentor can also provide a link with parents/carers. The Code of Practice places considerable emphasis on the importance of strong links between the school and home.

"The relationship between parents/carers of children with special educational needs and the school which their child is attending has a crucial bearing on the child's educational progress and the effectiveness of any school-based action." (DfE, 94)

A Way Forward

It is regrettable that much of the good work that is in place in the primary sector with regards to the emotional curriculum is lost at the primary/secondary transfer stage. The circle time approach towards dealing with a range of issues is just one example of a successful strategy for working with pupils which may be continued with older students. It offers students an opportunity to develop personally. The programme operates very much as a starting point and it is up to individual teachers and schools to decide how the work may be developed based on their own needs and priorities. It does not claim to provide a solution or have all the answers to managing behaviour but rather to ask questions and open up debate to address pertinent issues. Schools may then further develop their own appropriate systems and strategies.

It is important that those students who have been involved in the group remain supported once the course has finished. For example it may be appropriate to involve the student on a mentoring scheme or to further involve parents/carers in working with the school to support the student. A decision may be taken to involve an outside agency to build on and develop the work that has already been initiated through the course. It is important that decisions regarding future support and provision for the student are based on his or her individual needs and that an individual approach is adopted for each child. The course provides an individual profile of each child's individual needs. This should form part of an action plan to address and meet these needs. It is essential that a flexible approach is adopted. It may be appropriate to reduce or adapt the curriculum for students and look at individual packages that might include work experience placements or courses at further education colleges.

Alongside adapting the curriculum, school staff will also need to ensure that students are allocated a consistent and appropriate level of listening time. The mentoring scheme allows for a weekly one to one session for each student participating in the programme. This process clearly allows for students to discuss concerns and worries and ensures that they have a confidential and safe forum in which to problem solve difficult situations. As stated previously, it is essential that such opportunities continue to be made available to students to ensure that their needs continue to be met.

Schools may consider making use of this approach in terms of developing a whole school 'listening time' policy and approach. This may have implications for whole school staff training re-counselling skills and related issues, the appointment of a school counsellor, the development of a peer counselling process, the review of the PSHE curriculum with consideration of further developing opportunities for listening environments, and appropriate resources and materials to be developed.

Success Criteria

The success of the course can be measured in the following areas:

- Removing the risk of exclusion.
- Causing the school to reflect critically on its own practices and to assess the level to which this may impact upon behaviour and the development of individual students.
- Causing the school to further assess the appropriateness of the curriculum. Is there a need to further develop opportunities to address the social and emotional curriculum and such initiatives as peer tutoring?
- A review of the school's Behaviour and Bullying Policy in order to further develop whole school approaches.
- To look at teachers' expectations of behaviour and identify any need for staff training in the areas of cultural, gender and social-class awareness.
- To develop in students a further/improved understanding of their own feelings and attitudes.
- To further increase the ability to reflect upon behaviour and the consequences of behaviour.
- To increase/develop empathy.
- To improve listening skills.
- To improve management of anger.
- To improve ability to deal positively with conflict inside and outside the classroom context.
- To improve self-esteem.
- To reduce fights/verbal attacks on others.

Session 1

Student Interviews

SESSION 1

One to One Session with Individual Students.

Individual Session   1 hour

Session one consists of a one to one session between each individual student and the course tutor. The session should last approximately 1 hour and result in the development of a collaborative ethos i.e. the student will have been prompted to focus upon what works rather than what is currently going wrong. Hopefully, the student should be able to define some basic goals and the means by which he/she may be able to achieve these.

The session needs to take place in a quiet (private) room and the students should be made aware that this is a 'confidential' activity i.e. the course tutor will not feedback the student's views to members of staff or other involved adults unless the student requests that this be done. The only 'obvious' exception to this rule would be if the students disclosed themselves to be at risk in some sense. This also needs to be clarified to the student at the start of the session.

The course tutor will record the students' responses in note form on the one to one interview format during individual meetings between the course tutor(s) and all the students in order to define and articulate current difficulties and future goals. Each meeting follows a solution focused brief therapy format which, as implied, attends primarily to the development of solutions rather than the exploration of problems. The session will also hopefully allow for some quality relationship building time for both the student and the course tutor(s). Part 1 of this form basically identifies the following:

Part 1

> a) What is currently going well for the student at school and any reasons for this?
> b) What is currently not going quite so well at school and any ideas as to why this is so?
> c) What is currently going well at home and any reasons for this?
> d) What is currently not going quite so well at home and any ideas as to why this is so?
> e) Any ideas the student has as to what kind of help/support he/she might need i.e. what would actually help?

Part 2

This part of the one to one interview format asks the student the so called 'miracle question'. The idea is for the student to imagine themselves in a situation where all their problems and difficulties are 'solved'. The student is required to describe a 'perfect' day in which everything, both at home and at school goes well for them. The question is phrased as follows:

> "Imagine that you go to bed tonight and a miracle happens someone or something waves a magic wand over you and all your problems and difficulties are solved. You wake up to a perfect day at home and at school. What is different? Have a THINK. How does your day begin and then go on?"

Talk through what happens on this ideal/magic day. The idea of presenting the 'miracle question' in the one to one initial interview is to enable students to begin to gain a vision of 'life without the problem' (de Shazer, 1988; Furman & Ahola, 1992). In talking about life without the problem, they may begin to develop a series of clues, suggestions and ideas as to how they might begin to change and to identify appropriate and achievable goals for themselves. The scaling activity then aims to provide a visual image for the student to identify where he/she is at and where and how they would like to go i.e. identify goals. The solution focused procedures made use of in this one to one initial interview are described in Rhodes and Ajmal's book 'Solution Focused Thinking in Schools'. As they state:

> "Working with behavioural difficulties in schools is one of the most challenging areas of our work. People often reach a state when they don't know what else they can do and the situation is often presented in terms of failure. In supporting students, teachers and parents in their wish to change what is happening, we have found no model of approaching behavioural difficulties more useful and flexible than solution focused thinking. It enables a different story to be told, one which emphasises the skills, strengths and resources of the involved. Furthermore, it is not an exclusive model and seems to combine successfully with other techniques."
>
> Rhodes, J. & Ajmal, Y. (1995)

When posing the miracle question it is important to emphasise to the student that this ideal/magic day does actually involve attending school (even if, at this point, he/she does not think school could ever get better). Once the students' responses to the 'miracle question' have been recorded it will then be possible to answer the next question: 'What is different to a 'usual' day'? The objective here is to identify the differences in order to then make an assessment/draw up a basic list of which things need to be changed and the resources needed to enable these changes to be made.

Some Examples

Fred - aged 14

Fred said that when he woke up in the morning his mum was always rushing and in a bad mood and frequently shouted at him. In his 'miracle day' his mum was smiling and happy in the morning. On reflection, Fred stated that his mum was probably in a bad mood because he did not get out of bed on time and he could not get up in the mornings because he was too tired. He was too tired because he was watching satellite TV until 1.30am. His mum was angry because he was so lazy and she felt stressed because she had to get out to work in the morning and he was not helping her.

In order to make the appropriate changes Fred agreed that he needed to do the following:

- Buy his own alarm clock.

- Set the alarm for 20 minutes earlier than he was currently doing.

- Watch satellite TV on Fridays and Saturdays and keep it off during week nights.

- Get to bed by 10.30pm Mondays - Thursdays.

- Get his own breakfast and wash up afterwards.

Carla - aged 13

Carla said that she just could not get on with her maths teacher and that this had started in year 7 when she first entered secondary school. She couldn't seem to do anything right and she was always being accused of shouting out or disrupting the lesson when really it was other people who were doing these things. In her 'miracle day' the maths teacher was smiling and saying 'well done' and she was really good at maths.

On reflection, Carla stated that she did tend to chat a lot in the maths lessons because she found the work so hard and this made her feel 'stupid'. She was frightened to ask the teacher for help in case the others called her 'dumb'. Carla recognised that the maths teacher was fed up with her and thought that she was a 'pain'.

In order to make the appropriate changes Carla agreed that she needed to do the following:

- Sit at the front of the class, nearer to the teacher and next to a sympathetic and sensitive member of the class who could help her if she got stuck.

- Try not to get so worked up / be so 'loud' in class.

- Go and see the maths teacher privately to say that she was finding things difficult and ask for more help.

- Carla also agreed that the course tutor could talk to the maths teacher and feedback to him how much she wanted to 'get on' and recognise that she needed more help. She would also like to receive more praise for doing the 'right' thing.

These examples are based on real-life interviews but obviously names have been changed in order to ensure anonymity.

Answering this second question in part 2 of the one to one interview then enables the student to complete the scaling activity (Part 3). It is this activity which will hopefully allow students to measure their own progress and achievements at the end of the 10 week course, when this scaling process is repeated.

Part 3

The Scaling Activity

Students are required to rate themselves on a scale of 0-10. (0 would imply that they feel extremely negative about life and their school experience, 5 would imply that they feel okay about life and their school experience but recognise the need to make improvements, 10 would imply that all aspects of life could not get better i.e. perfection!)

This scale/rating system clearly needs to be explained to students at the start of the activity. Once a rating has been recorded, students can reflect further on the brief therapy process and identify the following:

- Why I am where I am now on the scale?

- Where I would like to be?

- How I can get there i.e. what do my own personal targets have to be?

Students should be given a photocopy of the scaling activity so that they can refer to this in reinforcing personal goals and the means by which they aim to achieve success.

- I am on a 4.

- This is because I am in trouble with teachers quite a lot for being disruptive and I am behind with my coursework and my mum is fed up with me.
- I would like to be on 8 or 9.

I can get there if I try these targets:

√ Sit on my own away from people I chat to.
√ Go to Homework Club and do my work.
√ Make a catch up timetable for coursework.
√ Only go out at weekends not in the week.
√ Think before I answer back the teachers.

RESOURCES

The following resources will be needed for the one to one interviews:

- A quiet (private) room.

- 1 hour approximately per student.

- Photocopy of the Brief Therapy Format.

- Photocopy of the Scaling Activity Format.

Crucial Skills

1:1 Interview

Name
Year Group
School
Course Tutor

Part 1

a) What is currently going well for you at school? Why?

b) What is currently not going quite so well at school? Why?

c) What is currently going well at home? Why?

d) What is not going quite so well at home? Why?

e) What do you think might help you at school?

f) What do you think might help you at home?

Part 2

a) The Miracle Question

Imagine that you go to bed tonight and a miracle happens - someone or something waves a magic wand over you and all your problems and difficulties are solved.

You wake up to a 'Perfect Day' at home and at school.

What is different? Have a THINK. How does your day begin and then go on?

Talk through what happens on this miraculous day.

What is different to a 'usual' day? Let's think back and list the differences.

Usual Day	Miraculous Day
•	
•	
•	
•	
•	
•	
•	
•	

Part 3

The Scaling Activity

Name: _____

Year Group: _____

School: _____

Mark where you are now.

I am at point

What have you done to get as far as that?

I have done these things:

- •

- •

- •

- •

- •

Where would you like to be?

I would like to reach point...

How can you get there?

My targets to reach that point are:

⇒

⇒

⇒

⇒

⇒

(0)
(1)
(2)
(3)
(4)
(5)
(6)
(7)
(8)
(9)
(10)

Session 2

Building Student Profiles

SESSION 2

- Crucial Skills Questionnaire.
- Development of Individual Student Profile.

Group Session 45 minutes - 1 hour

All students will be required to complete the responses. In Parts 1 and 2 responses can be made by ticking the appropriate point on a scale whilst those in Part 3 of the questionnaire demand only short answers/sentences.

It will be important at the start of the session to reinforce the purpose of this course to all students. Objectives might be as follows:

- To give students a time and private 'group' space to reflect on their own behaviour and the consequences of their behaviour.

- To help students develop their own self help strategies in order to manage and control anger and strong feelings.

- To encourage students to identify situations of potential conflict and withdraw from them as appropriate.

- To build up their confidence.

- To increase their ability to co-operate in a group, and to support and empathise with others.

It will also be necessary to point out the importance of completing the essential skills questionnaire as honestly and seriously as possible since this form clarifies exactly where the student is now; in terms of attitude, behaviour and ability to cope with angry feelings and confrontation, alongside reinforcing personal targets. Students are given a second opportunity to make use of the scaling activity (in the final reflection- particularly regarding ability to cope effectively with anger/conflict situations, they may wish to formulate new targets or further develop existing ones).

The questionnaire requires students to rate themselves on the following:

- Working in class in all curriculum areas.

- Homework in all curriculum areas.

- Getting on with peers in all curriculum areas.

- Getting on with the teacher in all curriculum areas.

- Punctuality.

- Attendance.

- Social skills.

- Attitude towards self.

- Attitude towards school.

- Behaviour toward other pupils.

- Attitude towards home life/situation.

- Behaviour in comparison to others in peer group.

It also requires students to assess when and where they are most likely to get into trouble in school and to identify possible reasons for this and current trend strategies that they might (sometimes) be using in order to cope in such situations. They also have the opportunity to identify what currently tends to make them feel angry and how they react to others when they are angry.

The responses to the questionnaire then allow course tutor and students to draw up a student profile (after the session is completed) which basically summarises the responses and identifies key areas of concern. (See pages 32 - 34) For example, it may well be the case that a student has a particular difficulty or 'clash' with a member of staff/a small group of staff. This problem may have been building up slowly over a number of terms/years and finally resulted in a state of impasse i.e. the student dislikes the teacher who he/she feels does not like them and has labelled them as 'bad' and the teacher is totally fed up with having their lessons disrupted by a student with whom he/she is rapidly losing patience or any sense of goodwill.

The student profile should consequently allow:

- The student to reflect on what he/she is/isn't doing 'right' and attempt to work out a series of targets or strategies in order to cope better in these particular lessons.

- The course tutor to make contact with the teacher (given permission by agreement with the student) and to enlist support via the formulation of a 'behaviour amnesty' i.e. the teacher is aware of what the student is attempting to do in order to change and cope better and he/she agrees to reflect further regarding the possibility of moving away from confrontation with this pupil and attempting a more positive approach.

The teacher will need to agree not to discuss this matter with other members of staff/ in front of other pupils and to meet privately with the student in order to give and gain feedback and assess progress re: the whole situation.

RESOURCES

- A quiet room with adequate seating and tables.

- Pens, pencils, rubbers.

- 45 minutes - 1 hour to run the session.

- Photocopies of the crucial skills questionnaire for each student.

- 1 - 2 hours for course tutors to read through responses and formulates student profiles. Copies of these can then be handed over to students to allow for them to further reflect and consider ways forward/ useful strategies/ things that might help them to cope more positively.

Crucial Skills Questionnaire

Your attitudes

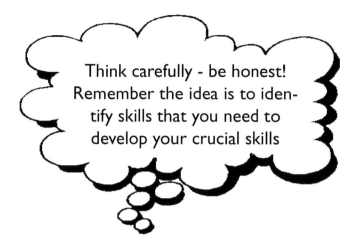

Think carefully - be honest!
Remember the idea is to identify skills that you need to
develop your crucial skills

Rate Yourself   Part 1

How do you think you are doing at the moment in the following subject areas? (Rate yourself out of 10 marks: 1 = poor and 10 = brilliant).

	Working in class	Homework	Getting on with peers	Getting on with teacher
English				
Science				
Technology				
Maths				
R.E.				
Geography				
Art				
History				
Business Studies				
Media Studies				
P.E.				

Part 2

Rate Yourself Out of 10

Punctuality

| 1 | 2 | 3 | 4 | 5 | 6 | 7 | 8 | 9 | 10 |

Poor   **Brilliant**

Attendance

| 1 | 2 | 3 | 4 | 5 | 6 | 7 | 8 | 9 | 10 |

Poor   **Brilliant**

Getting on with
others (social skills)

| 1 | 2 | 3 | 4 | 5 | 6 | 7 | 8 | 9 | 10 |

Poor   **Brilliant**

Attitude towards self
(self esteem/confidence)

| 1 | 2 | 3 | 4 | 5 | 6 | 7 | 8 | 9 | 10 |

Poor   **Brilliant**

Attitude towards
School

| 1 | 2 | 3 | 4 | 5 | 6 | 7 | 8 | 9 | 10 |

Poor   **Brilliant**

Behaviour towards
other pupils

| 1 | 2 | 3 | 4 | 5 | 6 | 7 | 8 | 9 | 10 |

Poor   **Brilliant**

Attitude towards
home life/situation

| 1 | 2 | 3 | 4 | 5 | 6 | 7 | 8 | 9 | 10 |

Poor   **Brilliant**

How do you think your
behaviour compares to
others in your year group?

| 1 | 2 | 3 | 4 | 5 | 6 | 7 | 8 | 9 | 10 |

Worse   **Average**   **Better**

Part 3

Anger Management/Problem Solving

1   How often do you get into trouble in school? (make an estimate/guess for one week)

_____

2   In which lessons do you generally tend to get into trouble?

_____

3   Why do you think this is?

_____

_____

4   What do you currently try and do in order to avoid getting into trouble?

_____

_____

5   Is there anything else that you can think of which might help you to stay out of trouble?

_____

_____

6   How can you help yourself?

_____

_____

7   How often do you tend to get into trouble out of school? (make an
     estimate/guess for 1 week)

_____

_____

8   What sort of things/situations cause you most difficulty?
     Why?

_____

_____

9   What do you do to try and help yourself in such situations?

_____

_____

10   What generally makes you feel angry? (give as many examples as you
     can).

_____

_____

11   What do you tend to do/ how do you tend to react to others when you feel angry?

_____

_____

_____

12   What do you think that you can do to help yourself in such situations?

_____

_____

_____

_____

13   Is there anyone else who might help you?

_____

14   What do you think you might get out of this particular course?

_____

15   What kinds of skills do you think that you need to develop in order to increase your current ratings?

_____

_____

Rate Yourself Overall

Mark a cross on the number you currently feel most represents how you feel about your life and how you are coping both in and out of school.

| 1 | 2 | 3 | 4 | 5 | 6 | 7 | 8 | 9 | 10 |

Bad   Medium   Fantastic

Then complete the following:

I gave myself_____ because I feel _____

Look to the Future
Set Your Targets

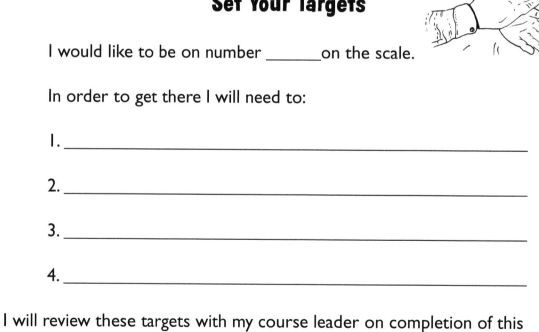

I would like to be on number _____on the scale.

In order to get there I will need to:

1. _____

2. _____

3. _____

4. _____

I will review these targets with my course leader on completion of this course.

Signed   _____

Date   _____

Summary Profile

Name _____

Problem Areas

◊

◊

◊

◊

Triggers

◊

◊

◊

◊

Current Strategies for Managing

◊

◊

◊

◊

Current Targets

◊

◊

◊

◊

Summary Profile

Name   Alexia Marsh

Problem Areas

◊ Science   Attitude towards teachers

◊ Punctuality

◊ Attitude towards school

◊ Behaviour in school

Triggers

◊ People disrespecting my mother

◊ People shouting

◊

◊

Current Strategies for Managing

◊ Keep my mouth shut.

◊ Set myself targets

◊ Count to 10

◊ Think before I take my actions

Current Targets

◊ Get to school on time

◊ Calm myself down

◊

◊

Summary Profile

Name _Christopher Grant_

Problem Areas

◊ English

◊ Science

◊ Attitude towards self

◊ Attitude towards home/life situation

Triggers

◊ People looking for trouble with me, mainly trying to get me into trouble

◊ Teachers judging me before the lesson and just thinking that I will be bad

◊

Current Strategies for Managing

◊ I am trying to explain to them how I feel, mainly just hope they understand and not judge me

◊ Keep my feelings to myself and not show my anger

◊

Current Targets

◊ Concentrate

◊ Give 100% to lessons

◊ Try to get along with the teachers

◊ Try stopping being bad and mucking around

Summary Profile

Name   Yusuf Mohamed

Problem Areas

◊   Homework

◊   Confidence

◊   Aggression

◊

Triggers

◊   Being on my own

◊   Losing my homework book

◊

◊

Current Strategies for Managing

◊   Pretending I don't care

◊   Keeping silent

◊

◊

Current Targets

◊   Ask for help from tutor

◊   Join homework club

◊

◊

Session 3

Setting the Circle

and

Triggers to Anger

SESSION 3

- Identifying Triggers to Anger.
- Setting Group Circle Rules.
- Articulating Needs.

Group Session 45 minutes - 1 hour

This session is divided into 3 main sections as follows:

1. Identifying Triggers to Anger

Students will be required to individually complete the brainstorming sheet 'What Makes me Feel Angry?' Course tutors will need to emphasise the importance of having an honest approach to this activity i.e. this is truly what makes me feel angry and encourage students to identify both school and home based situations. This activity needs to be completed without any consultation with other members of the group i.e. to ensure against plagiarism/students not really making a personal effort to identify their own needs. Comments can be written directly onto the brainstorming sheet.

2. Setting Group Circle Rules

Students will then be asked to form a circle and to feedback regarding what makes them feel angry to the rest of the group. However, prior to this it is essential that course tutors set up and agree group circle rules in order to protect the self-esteem of all individuals involved and to encourage a real sense of empathy and of the group being a support structure for students. Such rules might include:

- Everyone can have a say and is allowed to have a say.
- Everyone should respect and listen to each other.
- No one should laugh at/ridicule what others say.
- Do not break the confidential circle i.e. this is private and should not be discussed outside of the circle.
- We should all try to help each other to find real solutions.

Copies of agreed rules need to be given to all involved in these sessions. Prior to the start of this activity, it will also be necessary for students to observe the following rule, 'NO NAMES!' This means that if there is a particular problem with a particular teacher, then this needs to be discussed with a course tutor/SENCo/mentor/head of year on a private basis not in the context of the group. However clearly such issues can be raised. It is simply a matter of appropriately phrasing the problem. e.g. 'Miss Jackson shouts in my face and I get angry' should be phrased as 'I get angry if teachers shout in my face.'

All students can have the opportunity to feedback on the brainstorming activity prior to the final section of the session.

3. Articulating Needs

Again, this can be done in the circle. Students are simply required to state when and where they think they need the most help in order to control anger/deal with situations of conflict. The course tutors can reinforce the similarities in these situations and empathise how these feelings are common to all of us. It is the way in which we actually handle them that is crucial to our success and/or survival in the social situation. Students need now to be prompted to think of 'alternative' ways of sharing anger and ways of controlling anger in some of these situations.

RESOURCES

The following resources will be required for this session:

- A quiet room with adequate seating and tables.

- A pre-set circle of comfortable chairs.

- 45 minutes-1 hour.

- Photocopies of the brainstorming sheet for each student.

- A3 paper to record agreed circle rules / whiteboard and pens (course tutors to act as scribes).

- Access to a photocopier to ensure that all students receive a copy of the agreed rules.

- Pens, pencils, rubbers.

What Makes Me Angry?

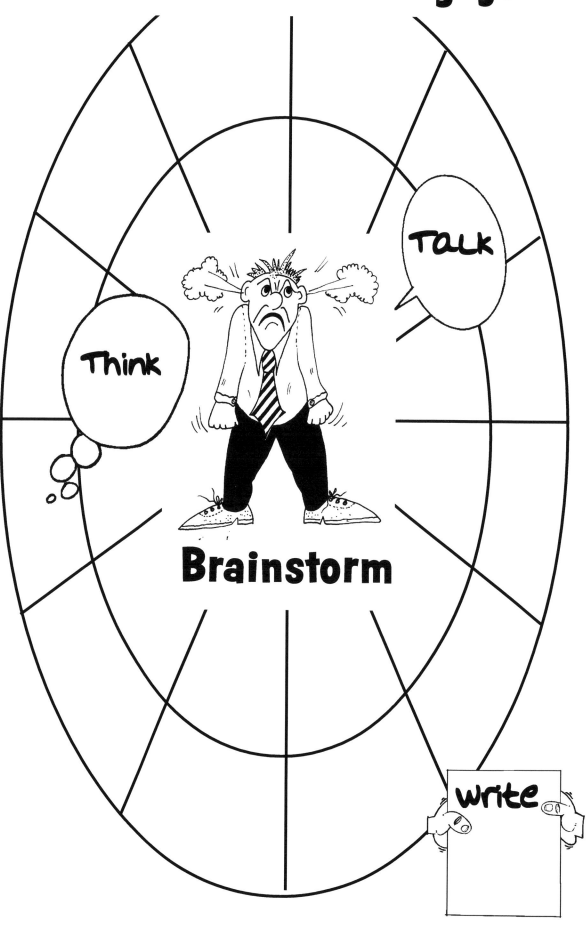

Think

Talk

Brainstorm

write

Example of Circle Rules

- ◆ **Everyone is allowed and encouraged to have their say.**

- ◆ **Everyone should respect and listen to each other.**

- ◆ **No one should ridicule another student.**

- ◆ **What we say in the circle is confidential so no shouting off about it!**

- ◆ **Everyone should try and help each other by building on our ideas and working out the best solutions and ways forward.**

Our Circle Rules

◆

◆

◆

◆

◆

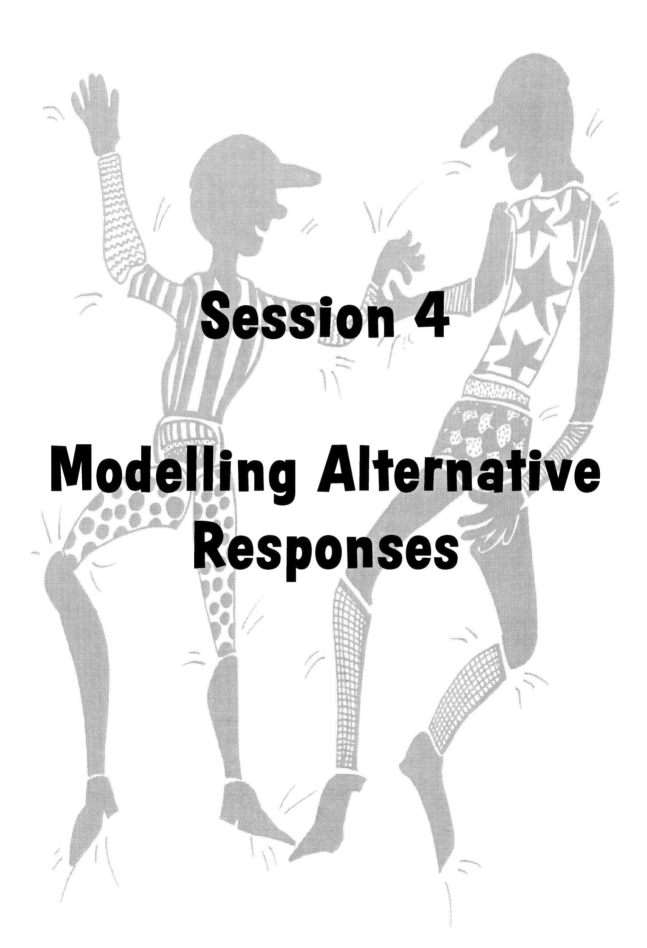

Session 4

Modelling Alternative Responses

SESSION 4

- Use of Situation Cards/Problem Cards Reflecting Triggers to Anger.
- Role Play and Modelling of Alternative Responses (by course tutors).

Group Session 45 minutes - 1 hour

This session is divided into 3 main sections as follows:

1. Feedback from the Course Tutors

Course tutors will have devised a list of situations which pupils identified in the previous session as being 'triggers' to anger. This list can be distributed to each student at the start of the session and course tutors may be able to identify certain common themes amongst the examples. e.g. threats to self-esteem, not getting your own way, insults to family, when you feel that people are not listening to you.

It will be important to emphasise how everybody experiences a range of problems both at home and at school. It is not just this group of students who will be experiencing these kind of difficulties and, in fact, adults are equally vulnerable to others threatening their self-image/not taking them seriously and not listening to their point of view.

In order to reinforce this point, it would be helpful to present students with a list of things that students have said make them feel angry, i.e. on previous Crucial Skills courses.

Your list might look like this:

Things That Students Say That Make Them Feel Angry

- When I do my homework and no one else does it and they don't get into trouble
- When I get homework
- When teachers put my name before me
- When I finish with a girl
- When I finish my work and the teachers give me even more
- When someone 'grasses me up'
- When I am playing football and I get fouled
- When I get the blame for something I didn't do
- When I am not allowed out
- When I get a detention and the teacher says you can do this and this in detention
- When someone messes about with me
- People are rude about what race you are

- When people 'cuss' my family and friends
- If people don't look the same as others and they get 'cussed'
- When people 'cuss' the clothes other people wear because they are jealous
- When people say you did something you didn't do
- When people hit you for no reason at all
- When people fight for no reason and one of them gets hurt
- When people give me dirty looks for no reason
- Discrimination
- I get 'cussed' because I am fat
- People try to trip you up
- When young kids get picked on by older kids
- When I get told off for something I didn't do
- When teachers tell me to shut up or that I am dumb and I can't say it back
- It makes me angry when I am bored
- When the teachers pay more attention to the 'boffins'
- When I have to do everything at home and my brother/sister doesn't have to
- When teachers think that people who do good work can't be bad
- When teachers say something bad to me and I say something bad to them and I get a detention
- When the teacher starts shouting at me for something I didn't do
- When people blame anything on me
- When a teacher picks on me for doing something little
- Taking the blame for my brother/sister
- When nobody listens to me
- When my brother starts crying when I am watching TV.

2. Problem Cards and Role Play Activity

Course tutors will then hand out copies of the 'problem card' format and explain that they have chosen one of the scenario detailed in the previous sessions. There is a role-play activity to 'act out'. The problem card describes the situation that causes the student to feel angry and then asks two questions as follows:

1 How do you currently deal with this?
2 How could you deal with this more positively?

The card then requests that students 'act out' the situation devising both a positive and negative way of dealing with it. Course tutors can explain that students will role play situations (and these scenes will be recorded via a video camera) in the next session. In this session, tutors will aim to model the activity (and the behaviours) for students. For example, one tutor can take on the role of the student whilst the other takes on the role of the teacher. The student is late for a lesson and doesn't have the appropriate equipment for the lesson. The teacher tackles the student and the student retaliates with verbal abuse, eventually leaving the room without permission (i.e. loss of temper). This would be 'acted out' first and must be done with utter conviction! This is clearly the 'negative' way of dealing with it. The tutors then 'act out' the 'positive way' i.e. the student is still late but manages to salvage the situation with a quiet, brief apology and by sitting down quickly and being honest about not having the right equipment.

3. Student Evaluation/Comments

Students will then be asked to comment upon the two scenes (be warned your acting skills will be under the microscope so do try hard!). A list of 'things to observe' can be given to the students at the start of the activity in order to prompt and guide their comments and observations. These may include:

- What went wrong?
- Why did the student in the first scene 'blow it'?
- Why did the teacher react in such an angry manner?
- What do you think the consequences will be in scene 1?
- What was different in scene 2?
- What did the student do to calm the situation?
- How did this make the tutor react?
- Was it 'easy' for the student to calm down? How did he/she manage to do this?

Students can make use of the circle structure to feedback to tutors. At the end of the session students will need to identify the situations that they would like to 'act out' in the next session and to clarify groups/pairs for this activity. This can be recorded by the course tutors to ensure ease of organisation at the start of the next session (notwithstanding any student absences).

Resources

The following resources will be required for this session:.

- A quiet room with adequate seating and tables and space for role play activity.

- A prearranged circle of comfortable chairs.

- 45 minutes - 1 hour to run the session.

- Photocopies of students' responses to the brainstorming activity 'Things That Make Me Feel Angry' and a 'Things That Students Say Make Them Feel Angry' list for each student.

- Photocopies of the problem card format. One of which will have been completed by course tutors ready for the role play activity.

- Photocopies of the 'Things to Observe' list for each student.

- Pens, pencils, rubbers.

Things to Observe
LOOK, THINK & REFLECT

Crucial Skills - Session 4
Course tutors' Role Play

Scene 1

What went wrong?

Why did the student in the first scene "blow it"?

Why did the teacher react in such an angry manner?

What do you think the CONSEQUENCES will be?

Scene 2

What was different?

What did the student do to calm the situation?

How did this make the teacher react?

Was it "easy" for the student to calm down?

How did he/she manage to do this?

Example - Things That Students Say That Make Them Feel Angry

- When I do homework and no one else does and they don't get into trouble
- When I get homework
- When teachers put my name before me
- When I finish with a girl
- When I finish my work and the teachers give me even more
- When someone 'grasses me up'
- When I am playing football and I get fouled
- When I get the blame for something I didn't do
- When I am not allowed out
- When I get a detention and the teacher says you can do all this in detention
- When someone messes about with me
- People are rude about what race you are
- When people 'cuss' my family and friends
- If people don't look the same as others and they get 'cussed'
- When people 'cuss' the clothes other people wear because they are jealous
- When people say you did something you didn't do
- When people hit you for no reason at all
- When people fight for no reason and one of them gets hurt
- When people give me dirty looks for no reason
- Discrimination
- I get 'cussed' because I am fat
- People try to trip you up
- When young kids get picked on by older kids
- When I get told off for something I didn't do
- When teachers tell me to shut up or that I am dumb and I can't say it back
- It makes me angry when I am bored
- When the teachers pay more attention to the 'boffins'
- When I have to do everything at home and my brother/sister doesn't
- When teachers think that people who do good work can't be bad
- When teachers say something bad to me and I say something bad to them and I get a detention
- When the teacher starts shouting at me for something I didn't do
- When people blame anything on me
- When a teacher picks on me for doing something little
- Taking the blame for my brother/sister
- When nobody listens to me
- When my brother starts crying when I am watching TV.

Example PROBLEM CARD

I get angry when

I arrive late for lessons and the teacher shouts at me

and doesn't give me a chance to speak.

Think! How do you currently deal with this?

I shout back and kick my chair or sometimes I walk out

of the lesson.

How could you deal with this more positively?

Not shout back

Sit down quietly

Apologise for being late

Act out the situation and devise both a positive and negative way of dealing with it.

PROBLEM CARD

I get angry when

_____

_____

_____

_____

Think! How do you currently deal with this?

_____

_____

_____

_____

How could you deal with this more positively?

_____

_____

_____

_____

Act out the situation and devise both a positive and negative way of dealing with it.

PROBLEM CARD

I get angry when

_____

_____

_____

_____

Think! How do you currently deal with this?

_____

_____

_____

_____

How could you deal with this more positively?

_____

_____

_____

_____

Act out the situation and devise both a positive and negative way of dealing with it.

Session 5

Developing Skills
Using Video

SESSION 5

- Use of Problem Cards Detailing Triggers to Anger.
- Student's Role Play Activities.
- Use of Video Recorder to Record Each Group's Two Scenes.

Group Session 45 minutes - 1 hour

This session is divided into 3 main sections as follows:

1. Feedback from the Previous Session

This will be required in order to clarify the groups and chosen situations for the role play activities. A list of the situations can also be provided for students in the event of any group/pair wishing to change their choice of scene. A suggested list can be found in resources for this session. A blank copy of the problem card will also need to be provided to students in order to enable them to record their final choice of scene for the role play activity.

It would also be a good idea to reinforce the 'circle rules' as these will doubtless apply to the co-operative work situation engendered by role play/ drama activities. Students should have a copy of these in their crucial skills folders for easy reference. Basically, students will all need to agree to the following:

- Think.

- Use your imagination.

- Do not criticise others' ideas/laugh at them.

- Work together and build upon each others' ideas.

- Students will need at least 10 minutes to work out and then practise the two scenes.

2. Role Play Activity

Each group will present their two scenes - one in which the student gets angry and responds in a negative way to a situation and one in which he/she encounters the same situation but responds in a positive way i.e. does not lose it. Course tutors will ask each group to present their scenes to the whole group and then ask for students to comment on each others work (bearing in mind the 'Things to Observe List' made use of in the previous session when viewing the tutor's role play). Each scene will be filmed in order to view and further evaluate in the next session. Students feedback on each others work might include comments on:

- What was different in the second scene?

- What was the point of 'conflict'?

- How did the student react more positively in the second scene?

- How do you think they managed to control their angry feelings?

Brief notes could be made on the comments sheet which suggests further appropriate questions and asks students to reflect upon what they have been watching.

3. Tutor Feedback

Finally, course tutors can highlight similarities in the scenes and positive ways of dealing with conflict/and anger that each scene has portrayed. All students should be praised for further developing their skills and listening to each other and sharing ideas. At this point, it might be a good idea for course tutors to reiterate how important it is for students to talk and share ideas. Talk is clearly powerful and sharing problems can initially reduce stress and then allow for solutions to be formulated. All of us are capable of thinking and reflecting upon behaviour and events and by doing this we can help ourselves, and others, to change. A possible means of reinforcing this is by brainstorming as a group in order to formulate a list of reasons as to why working in a group on such issues is of real value. An example of such a list can be found in the resources for this session.

RESOURCES

The following resources will be required for this session:

- A quiet room with adequate seating and tables and a space for practising and performing the role play activities.

- 45 minutes - 1 hour to run the session.

- Photocopies of the 'list of situations' for all students.

- Photocopies of blank 'problem cards' for each group.

- Video camera to record scenes.

- Photocopies of comments sheets for each student.

- Whiteboard/A3 paper and pens to use in formulating 'The Group is Good' list.

- Pens, pencils and rubbers.

- Relevant props for scenes e.g. bags, books, pens, hats, etc.

A list of Situations for the Problem card

- ♦ When a new teacher knows of me being a "bad kid" and they don't treat you how they treat the rest of the class.

- ♦ When people cuss/insult me.

- ♦ When people judge me without knowing me.

- ♦ People not seeing things from my point of view.

- ♦ The pressure of doing something I don't want to do.

- ♦ When people have something against me and they want to put me down.

- ♦ When I am doing well and people know that, but they want me to do bad.

- ♦ When the teacher makes little things into big things.

Problem Card

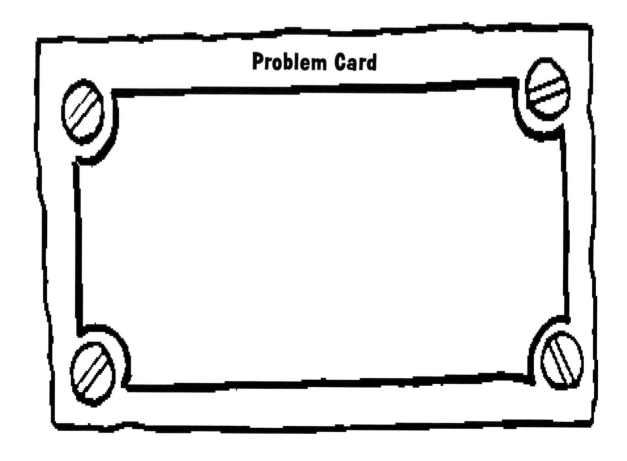

Problem Card

Comments Sheet

Think about the differences

Scene 1

♦ Why did this situation get out of hand?

♦ What did the student do? Why?

♦ What was the 'point of conflict' i.e. the moment when the situation just got too hot?

Scene 2

♦ How did the student react differently in the second scene?

♦ What impact did the student's behaviour have on the teacher?

♦ How do you think the student managed to control his/her angry feelings?

♦ Did the 'actors' LISTEN to each other more in Scene 1 or Scene 2? Did this help? Why?

Comments

Example - The Group is Good

Because...

♦ Talking is a powerful tool.

♦ We can share problems when we talk.

♦ If we stop, think and talk then we might not hit out.

♦ Talking about a problem reduces stress.

♦ We can support each other to find solutions.

♦ We can build friendships and make each other feel okay.

♦ We can reflect on our feelings and behaviours.

♦ We can help each other to cope with problems and anger by sharing ideas.

♦ We can help each other to change and be successful.

♦ We can help each other to feel happy.

Session 6

Identifying Effective Strategies

SESSION 6

- Viewing Role Plays.
- Completion of Review Form and Feedback.
- Starting to Identify Personal Strategies.

Group session 45 minutes - 1 hour

This session is divided into 3 main sections as follows:

1. Viewing the Role Plays

The first viewing will be purely for fun i.e. to allow students to recover from seeing themselves on the TV screen! The course tutors will then need to rewind the tape in order to allow for a second viewing. During this viewing, tutors can stop the tape at the end of each scene in order to allow students to complete the observation check list. Students will need to complete a checklist for each group that they observe in order to feedback and make appropriate comparisons at the end of the session.

2. Review Forms and Feedback

Students can feedback their comments regarding each group's scenes in the circle. Tutors will need to prompt and/or highlight the similarities or differences between the scenes and the strategies that students may have used to cope more effectively in the second scene. The review forms focus on:

- Identifying what went wrong.
- Identifying if student needed to 'show off' in order to 'save face' amongst the peer group.
- Identifying if the student's negative behaviour influenced the teacher's responses (and vice versa).
- Identifying if the characters actually listened to each other.
- Identifying if the consequences were good or bad.

Hopefully, this activity will again reinforce to students how easily situations can escalate and how they themselves do have the power to stop such a process or 'save the situation'. Most importantly, there should now be an increased awareness as to how stopping, reflecting and listening to both ourselves and others can make a very real difference to most situations.

3. Starting to Identify Personal Strategies

Students can spend the final 10 minutes of the session on an individual activity which requires them to reflect upon the strategies that they are currently making use of in order to manage angry feelings. A format for this activity can be found in the resources section of this session plan. This activity also prepares students for the focus on developing self-help strategies in the next session.

RESOURCES

The following resources will be required for this session:

- A quiet room with adequate seating and tables.

- A video and television.

- Tape of role play session.

- Photocopies of the review form need to be available to all students. Students will need one form per group.

- Comfortable chairs arranged in a circle for feedback time.

- Photocopies of the 'Personal Strategies Sheet' must be provided for each student.

- Pens, pencils, rubbers.

Oh, yes, Very Good.

Review Form

Your were Brilliant!

It was OK, I Suppose.

Wonderful!

Comments	Scene 1 Tick/Cross	Scene 2 Tick/Cross
Student was doing the wrong thing at the start.		
Student answered the teacher back.		
Student was rude to the teacher.		
Student broke the school rules.		
Student was 'showing off' to appear big in front of classmates.		
Teacher got angry as a result of student's behaviour.		
Teacher shouted.		
Teacher went 'over the top'.		
Student listened to the teacher.		
Teacher listened to the student.		
The consequences were okay.		
The consequences were bad.		

Names of Actors

Name of Reviewer

Date

Personal Strategies Sheet

Session 6

How Do I Cope With

Feeling Angry?
Think! What are my Strategies?

- ◆
- ◆
- ◆
- ◆
- ◆

Which do I use the most?

In which situations do I need to make use of this strategy?

Why does it seem to work for me?

Personal Strategies Sheet

Session 6

How Do I Cope With

Feeling Angry?
Think! What are my Strategies?

♦

♦

♦

♦

♦

Which do I use the most?

In which situations do I need to make use of this strategy?

Why does it seem to work for me?

Session 7

Using Skills to Solve Conflict

SESSION 7

- Feedback Re-Personal Anger Management Strategies.
- Introduction of a Range of Strategies/Techniques. (Students may use to manage anger or problem solve conflict situations).
- Problem Page. Two Problems to Solve.

Group Session 45 minutes - 1 hour

This session is divided up into 3 main sections as follows:

1. Students' feedback

Talk to the group about the kinds of strategies that they are currently able to use in order to manage angry feelings and tricky or difficult situations. The Circle Rules will need to be reinforced in order to again ensure that all students feel comfortable in performing this activity and that they are valued for their honest contributions. Course tutors can also contribute in this session by discussing the strategies that they use in order to cope in conflict situations/when they feel angry. Hopefully there may well be some similarities in the strategies disclosed. These might include:

- Ignoring
- Deep breathing and relaxation techniques
- Positive thinking
- Being assertive and 'putting back' the anger onto the other person
- Walking away
- Thinking of something else
- Listening
- Speaking quietly
- Being firm but fair when you do not agree
- Thinking before you act/talk
- Saying 'I am angry, Help!'
- Using your friends for positive support.

2. A Range of Strategies

Course tutors can list the range of strategies that have been suggested by students (and themselves). A format is provided for this activity in the resources section of this session plan. After the session students should all be provided with a photocopy of this sheet when it has been completed and everyone has made at least one contribution (even if it is the same as someone else's).

Course tutors can then introduce a range of 'stepped' approaches to anger management which are all based on the visual image of traffic lights. Students can discuss the relative values of each method and perhaps begin to think about what sort of visual image they might make use of in order to develop a personal system of this kind. These strategies are as follows :

Strategy 1

Say it! - What is the problem?
Plan   - What can I do to sort it out? Who can help me?
Think! - How do I feel?

Step 1 - Ask the student to identify and then articulate the problem. This does not mean 'think in your head' but rather, to actually talk through the problem . Remember how powerful talk can be.

Step 2 - As usual, amber is the crucial colour in the traffic light sequence. This is the stage where the student identifies what he/she needs in order to solve a problem. This will include identifying the 'how' and the 'who' i.e. how can I do this and who can help me?

Step 3 - Students will then be able to identify how they feel once they have identified a solution i.e. relieved, happier, more able to cope.

Strategy 2

Stop - What is the problem?
Hold the hands - don't lash out.
Walk away - get yourself out of the situation. Go somewhere quiet and cool off.

Step 1 - Ask student to identify and articulate the problem i.e. say it out loud, think it aloud! The 'talking' is the most important means of affirming that there is a problem that needs to be dealt with.

Step 2 - Students may wish to use this 'hold the hands' strategy or another physical strategy to prevent an assault on another student. They may also wish to adopt a 'self talk' approach i.e. actually telling themselves not to lash out.

Step 3 - The 'GO' light here suggests that the student should move away and get themselves out of the difficult situation - again, this is a physical action and intended to diffuse a situation of conflict.

Strategy 3

Don't do it! Don't lash out!
What is wrong?
What can I do?

What will be the consequences?
Make a positive plan and try it out - BE POSITIVE!

Step 1 - The student should be encouraged to stop and avoid reacting to the problem in a negative way e.g. arguing back or hitting out, verbally or physically, at the other person. The student should be encouraged to make use of the visual imagery of the red traffic light calling a halt to any negative behaviour or reaction.

Step 2 - Again the crucial amber stage should enable the student to firstly identify what exactly is wrong/what is the problem. This needs to be articulated aloud. The longer that you are thinking and talking the less time you have to hit out. This stage also involves identifying the various options. The student will need to ask 'what can I do?' and also identify what the consequences would be of any action i.e. both positive and negative.

Step 3 - It is at this point that the student can identify the most positive plan and put it into action.

Strategy 4
Angry?
Someone upset you?
Something gone wrong?
Stop! Take a deep breath
Count in your head 10-20
Think positive
Go - let your breath out slowly
KEEP CALM
Make a plan - go for it!

Step 1 - The first step relies on the student actually having real self knowledge and being able to identify and label their own angry feelings. This will also involve articulating the cause of the problem whether it is a person or a particular situation.

Step 2 - The student needs to stop and stand still taking a deep breath. As the student is doing this he or she will need to mentally count to 10 or 20. This should enable the student to move on to the next step in a more positive frame of mind.

Step 3 - The student should slowly exhale, keeping really calm whilst attempting to identify the best way forward. This may involve making a plan or may simply involve walking away and seeking support from elsewhere.

3. Two Problems to Solve

Students can then attempt to transfer their own developing skills in order to help an 'imaginary' student who is apparently at risk of exclusion from secondary school. A 'problem page' letter can be found in the resources section and students will need individual copies of this letter in order for them to take on the role of agony aunt/uncle and compose an appropriate and useful response which indicates their growing awareness of useful and practical strategies. These responses can be fed back to the circle and students can compare and evaluate their answers.

Finally, students can spend the final 10 minutes of the session completing a 'personal problem sheet' in which they identify a current difficulty and formulate a series of appropriate strategies that they might consider using. These 'problems' do not need to be 'shared' in the circle and course tutors will need to make themselves available to students who require some one to one time in order to further discuss any issues arising from this activity.

RESOURCES

The following resources will be required for this session:

- A quiet room with adequate seating and tables.

- Students' copies of personal strategies sheet from the previous session.

- A copy of the group's anger management strategies sheet which is to be completed in the session (tutor acting as scribe). At the end of the session this will need to be photocopied to allow each student to have a personal copy for reference and reinforcement (place in file).

- Photocopies of the stepped approaches. Each student will require individual copies for their own reference and to place in their files.

- Photocopies of the problem page letter for each student.

- Paper for each student on which to formulate a letter in response to this problem.

- Photocopies of the personal problem sheet.

- Pens, pencils and rubbers.

- Comfortable chairs arranged in a circle for feedback time.

Our Group's
Anger Management Strategies

Names of Students:

Names of Tutors

Date Recorded

- ◆ We can

- ◆ We can

- ◆ We can

- ◆ We can

- ◆ We can

- ◆ We can

- ◆ We can

- ◆ We can

- ◆ We can

- ◆ We can

Anger Management Strategies
Stepped Approaches

Positive Thinking and Self Talk

Strategy 1

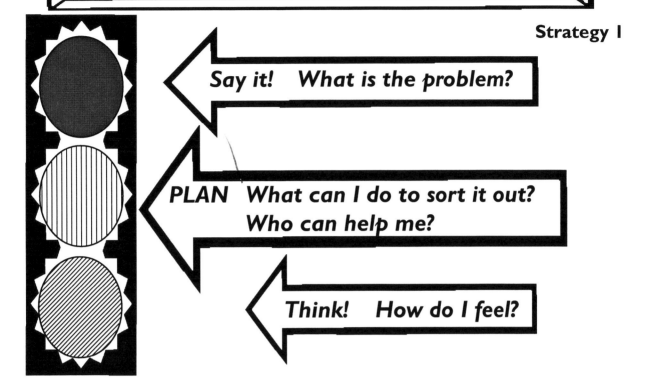

Say it!   What is the problem?

PLAN   What can I do to sort it out?
Who can help me?

Think!   How do I feel?

Strategy 2

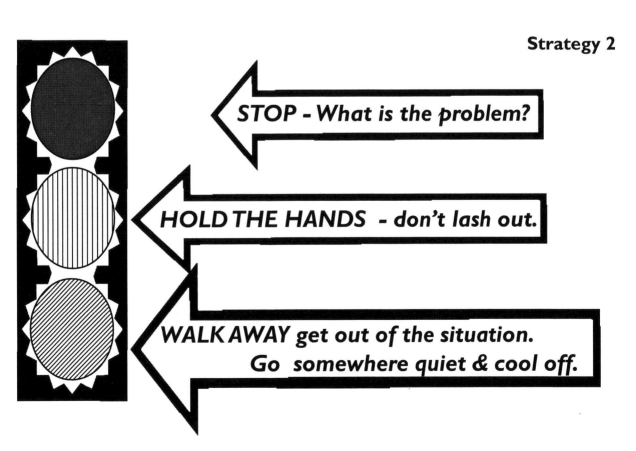

STOP - What is the problem?

HOLD THE HANDS - don't lash out.

WALK AWAY get out of the situation.
Go somewhere quiet & cool off.

Strategy 3

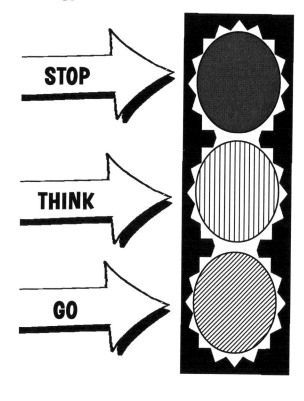

STOP

Don't do it!
Don't lash out!

THINK

What is wrong?
What can I do?
What are the consequences?

GO

Make a positive plan
Try it out-
Be POSITIVE!!

Strategy 4

ANGRY?
Someone upset you?
Something gone wrong?

STOP! Take a deep breath
Count in your head 10/20
Think positive

GO   Let out your breath slowly -
KEEP CALM -
Make a plan - go for it!

A Problem to Solve

Dear Daniel,

Can you help me? I'm so fed up. I'm in trouble all the time at school and it's got so bad that Mr. Harvey (Head of Year) has said one more chance and then I'll be excluded for good. I've already had 3 exclusions and Mum's giving me gries about it at home.

She said she's fed up and it's all my fault. She doesn't understand how I get so angry and wound up. All the teachers apart from two of them just don't give me a chance. They put my name before me all the time and show me up and make a fool of me.

Sometimes it gets so bad that I just shout back and then I make it worse. I feel like I've no way out because of my reputation. I want to get on but I just feel so angry and I'm worried that they won't give me a chance.

Can you help me?

Yours, Mel.

A Personal Problem Sheet

**What problem would you write
about to an Agony Aunt?**

**THINK!
How do you feel?
What is wrong?**

Look back and re-read your problem.

Can you think about some of the self-help strategies that we've talked
about on the course?

Can you work out some solutions/ideas for coping and list them?

I could:

♦

♦

♦

♦

♦

Session 8

New Solutions and New Strategies

SESSION 8

- More Problems to Solve.
- Further Role Plays. Looking for New Solutions/Strategies.
- Use of Video Recorder to Record Each Group's Two Scenes.

Group Session 45 minutes - 1 hour

This session is divided up into 3 main sections as follows:

1. More Problems to Solve

Students are presented with a series of problem cards (using the same format as session 4). These cards will have been completed by course tutors prior to the start of the session and will make use of students' contributions /ideas/feedback from previous sessions. The problem cards may reflect difficult situations that students are currently experiencing or have previously experienced, both in and out of the school context. However tutors will need to carefully phrase these situations/problems so as to ensure anonymity, i.e. they need to be set out in a 'generalised' way.

> e.g. 'I get angry when people make racist comments to me.'

> As opposed to:

> 'I get angry when Jason calls me a gorilla.'

A set of eight suggested problems are included in this lesson and these can be made use of if course tutors feel they are appropriate/fairly represent the concerns of their group of students. Course tutors can ask students for their initial responses to these problems making use of the circle approach and also reinforce the range of strategies introduced in the previous session alongside 'personal' strategies already being made use of by students. Most importantly, it is essential to reinforce the solution focused approach in which students can identify the problem rather than dwelling on it in a negative way, they can focus on developing solutions which work for them. For example, one student may have particular difficulty with an individual member of staff and this may result in a considerable focus on the negative aspects, e.g. 'He is so nasty. He shouts so much. He always shows me up. He laughs when I can't do the work. He makes me feel dumb. I hate him.' A major aim of this course is to translate these negative statements into positive strategies e.g. 'I can keep quiet and calm and try to listen in these lessons. I can talk to my form tutor and explain how I'm feeling. I can get some more help with the course work. I can ask my form tutor to talk to this teacher on my behalf.'

2. Role Plays

Students can make use of these problem cards to devise and act out the two alternative scenes. One in which the student does the 'wrong' thing and the other in which the student makes use of self-help strategies in order to cope in a more positive way with the particular problem. Students may need to be prompted again to really think about the 'best way' to react, i.e. the way which will result in a more positive outcome for them and to articulate exactly what it is that they are doing differently to ensure such an outcome. Students will need approximately 10-15 minutes to work co-operatively on these two scenes. Course tutors can then video each of the scenes as each group performs them to the rest of the group.

3. Circle Closure

Course tutors can then ask students to contribute a comment each in answer to the question 'How do the 'positive' scenes show the progress we're all making in solving problems and coping with anger?' This activity should provide an initial forum for students to further identify the skills they're now using and act out, as preparation for the next session.

RESOURCES

The following resources will be required for this session:

- A quiet room with adequate seating, tables and space to perform and practise the role plays.

- Students' Crucial Skills folders for reference (Range of strategies and personal strategies).

- Copies of situation cards in which problems will have been completed /entered in by course tutor(s).

- Comfortable chairs arranged in a circle for the circle closure time.

- Video recorder.

- Pens, pencils and rubbers (in the event of students wishing to make any notes/ plan role plays).

I get angry when people make racist comments to me.

I get angry when teachers blame me for doing something bad in the lesson and it wasn't me.

I get angry when the teacher tries to make me look stupid in front of the class.

I get angry when Mum believes the teacher and believes her when it wasn't my fault.

I get angry when the teacher doesn't explain the work properly and I can't do it because I don't understand it.

I get angry when people in my family leave me out of things.

I get angry when the work is too hard for me and I feel dumb.

I get angry when no one in my family has the time to listen to me or help me.

Session 9

Action Plans
and
Revisiting the Skills

SESSION 9

- Viewing of Video.
- Identification of Further Clarification of Skills.
- Devising an Action Plan for Carlos.

Group Session 45 minutes - 1 hour

This session is divided up into 3 main sections as follows:

1. Viewing and Analysing the Video

Students and course tutors can watch the role plays. The first viewing (as in session 6) can be purely for fun and allow time for students to recover, or otherwise, from seeing themselves on the screen. The course tutor(s) will then need to rewind the tape in order to allow for a second viewing. During this viewing, tutors can stop the tape at the end of each two scenes in order to allow students to complete the skills checklist. These will need to be completed at the end of each two scenes (i.e. for each two group's work) in order for students to feedback and make informed evaluations at the end of the viewing period. This process will also enable students to ask each other questions about the strategies they were using. e.g. Was I right? Were you trying to ignore the comment? Did you keep repeating in your head 'I won't let this get to me?' Were you thinking 'Just keep calm, don't blow it!'

2. Identification and Further Clarification of Skills

Students can feedback their comments regarding the scenes in the circle context and with reference to their completed skills checklists. The checklist focuses on increasing student's awareness of strategies that are being used by others and that they themselves can also make use of in the relevant/ similar contexts. Students can also have the opportunity to clarify with each other if their own observations of others behaviour/strategies were accurate.

3. Devising an Action Plan for Carlos

Students are next required to move from a focus on themselves and their own peer group and to transfer the skills that they have gained to date into 'solving' someone else's problem. Students will be presented with a brief 'Case History' of Carlos who is a fictional year 8 student at a local Secondary School. Carlos is experiencing difficulties in a number of areas but primarily in controlling his anger and in managing his behaviour in some areas of the curriculum. Students will be asked to read through the Case History and to discuss with a partner (or in a group of 3), the kinds of problems that Carlos is experiencing and to then identify a way forward for this pupil. The way forward will take the form of an action plan which will detail the following:

- Areas of difficulty.

- What need to change first.

- Setting targets.

- Advising on strategies/methods to support the targets.

- Setting a review date, i.e. a point/time at which to reflect on success and to set further targets as appropriate.

This activity should help to prepare students to develop their own action plans in the next session and also again reinforce the solution-focused approach to looking at and solving problems.

RESOURCES

The following resources will be required for this session:

- A quiet room with adequate seating and tables.

- Comfortable chairs arranged in a circle to allow for feedback for the skills checklist.

- A video and the tape of the role play session.

- Photocopies of the crucial skills checklist for each student (1 for each groups 2 scenes).

- A photocopy of the 'Case History' for each student.

- A photocopy of the 'Action Plan' for each student/group of students to complete.

- Pens, pencils, rubbers.

- Crucial skills folders for reference as appropriate.

CRUCIAL SKILLS
CHECKLIST

Name   **Date**

Look carefully! Think!
What skills do you think the student was using in the scene?
Use the Tick boxes. Make any additional comments at the end of the form.

I think that _____ **was:**

☐ Ignoring the problem/comments/other person.

☐ Walking away physically.

☐ Walking away mentally.

☐ Using relaxing technique e.g. deep breathing.

☐ Using a traffic light method.

☐ Using other stepped approach to coping with anger.

☐ Using 'Positive' thinking.

☐ Using assertion e.g. putting 'back' the anger onto the other person.

☐ Listening to and considering what the other person was saying.

☐ Thinking about the consequences.

☐ Stopping and thinking before.

☐ Responding calmly.

☐ Thinking of something better/more positive.

☐ Not worrying about what others might think, e.g. other students.

☐ Stopping to plan and think ahead.

☐ Acting 'in control'.

Other Strategies/Ideas

Case History

Case Notes

◊ In trouble with Maths teacher, Year 7 for shouting out in class and not sitting down and doing his work.

◊ Sent to HOY for hitting another boy in the Lunch Hall. Carlos reported that the other boy said he was a monkey and started to cuss his family and was making racist comments. The other boy also said that Carlos' Mum was an AIDs carrier. Both boys were suspended for 2 days.

◊ Put on report at the start of Year 8 because he had been so disruptive in both Maths and Science. Carlos said that the work was too hard for him but staff felt that he was just being lazy and needed to start concentrating.

◊ HOY phoned Mrs. Wright (Mum) to inform her that Carlos was significantly behind in his Maths and Science homework.

◊ Carlos swore at the Maths teacher and left the room without permission. He was given a double detention.

◊ 2 incidents reported of Carlos hurting 2 Year 7 boys in the playground. Carlos said that these 2 boys had called him 'dumb' when they walked past him in the corridor. The other boys denied this. Carlos was given a new report card and Mum was phoned. Mum was angry with Carlos but said she did not know what was wrong.

◊ 3 day exclusion for swearing at HOY.

Name of Student
Carlos Wright
D.o.B. 2.1.86
Year Group 8
School Barton Grange School

Action Plan

Name   Date

Year Group   School

Identifying the main areas of difficulty.

What needs to change first?

What should _____'s Targets be?

1. _____

2. _____

3. _____

4. _____

What strategies/resources does _____ need in order to achieve these targets?

*

*

*

*

When should this Action Plan be reviewed?

What changes should occur in _____'s behaviour between then and now?

Session 10

Evaluation and Looking Forward

SESSION 10

- Evaluation of the Programme.
- Developing Individual Action Plans.

Group Session 45 minutes - 1 hour

This session is divided into 3 main sections as follows:

1. Verbal Feedback

Students can be given the opportunity to feedback in the circle. Course tutor(s) can initially pose one basic question:

"What do you think you've gained from following this crucial skills course?"

This should prompt students to reflect on the content of the course and whether or not they have further developed their own skills in terms of coping with angry feelings and in dealing with conflict/difficult situations. The course tutor(s) will need to encourage students to think about anything that has changed for them by following the course and adopting self help strategies. This activity will prepare students ready to complete the evaluation form. Allow 15 minutes for the writing and 10-15 minutes for verbal feedback.

2. Evaluation Forms

Each student will require an individual copy of the form which mainly requires tick box responses. As this method makes for relative ease of recording, students should be able to respond in a more reflective and relaxed way. Each student will need a 'quiet space' in which to complete the form and course tutor(s) should request that all students work independently so as to ensure that it is their own responses that are recorded, not the responses of other members of the group! The evaluation form is divided into four sections which focus on the following areas:

- Enjoyment, usefulness and change ratings.

- Skills learned and put into practice.

- Identification of changes, personal and context.

- Contribution to future course planning.

Once students have completed the evaluation forms, they can be presented with formats for developing their own individual action plans.

3. Individual Action Plans

This final course activity requires students to reflect upon their own progress and then to develop a current action plan which they can work on/ towards over the following half-term period (or as appropriate).

This action plan focuses on the following:

- Identifying progress to date.

- Identifying remaining/current problem areas.

- Clarifying and formulating new and appropriate targets.

- Clarifying how these targets will be met, e.g. strategies and resources.

- Setting a date to review the plan and identifying success criteria.

A copy of this format should to be provided for each individual student and tutor(s) will need to make themselves available to support students in completion of the plans (as appropriate). Course tutors should also ensure that students are provided with a further one to one session, if requested, in order to ensure reinforcement of skills and strategies and a clear and positive picture of the way ahead.

RESOURCES

The following resources will be required for this session:

- A quiet room with adequate seating and tables.

- Comfortable chairs arranged in a circle to allow for verbal feedback on the course.

- A copy of the evaluation form for each student.

- A copy of the individual action plan form for each student.

- Crucial skills folders for students to refer to as appropriate.

- Pens, pencils, rubbers.

- A treat of biscuits, cakes and soft drinks for all members of the group and course tutors.

Crucial Skills Evaluation Form

Name   **Year Group**   **D.o.B.**

Date Course Started   **School**

Date Evaluation for Completed

Section 1 - Ratings

Give a mark out of 10 for the following aspects of the course.
Mark the scale with an arrow. 1 = poor and 10 = brilliant.

1 ___ 2 ___ 3 ___ 4 ___ 5 ___ 6 ___ 7 ↓ 8 ___ 9 ___ 10

Enjoyable

1 ___ 2 ___ 3 ___ 4 ___ 5 ___ 6 ___ 7 ___ 8 ___ 9 ___ 10

Useful to me

1 ___ 2 ___ 3 ___ 4 ___ 5 ___ 6 ___ 7 ___ 8 ___ 9 ___ 10

Made a difference to how I feel about myself - more positive

1 ___ 2 ___ 3 ___ 4 ___ 5 ___ 6 ___ 7 ___ 8 ___ 9 ___ 10

Made a difference to how I feel about others - peers

1 ___ 2 ___ 3 ___ 4 ___ 5 ___ 6 ___ 7 ___ 8 ___ 9 ___ 10

Made a difference to how I feel about teachers

1 ___ 2 ___ 3 ___ 4 ___ 5 ___ 6 ___ 7 ___ 8 ___ 9 ___ 10

Helped me to help myself stay out of trouble

1 ___ 2 ___ 3 ___ 4 ___ 5 ___ 6 ___ 7 ___ 8 ___ 9 ___ 10

Helped me to identify problems and cope better

1 ___ 2 ___ 3 ___ 4 ___ 5 ___ 6 ___ 7 ___ 8 ___ 9 ___ 10

Helped me to control my anger

1 ___ 2 ___ 3 ___ 4 ___ 5 ___ 6 ___ 7 ___ 8 ___ 9 ___ 10

Helped me to think of the consequences

1 ___ 2 ___ 3 ___ 4 ___ 5 ___ 6 ___ 7 ___ 8 ___ 9 ___ 10

Helped me to develop new ways to cope with problems

1 ___ 2 ___ 3 ___ 4 ___ 5 ___ 6 ___ 7 ___ 8 ___ 9 ___ 10

Shown me that I can change and help others to change

1 ___ 2 ___ 3 ___ 4 ___ 5 ___ 6 ___ 7 ___ 8 ___ 9 ___ 10

Shown me that talk is powerful and can help

1 ___ 2 ___ 3 ___ 4 ___ 5 ___ 6 ___ 7 ___ 8 ___ 9 ___ 10

Helped me to improve my behaviour

1 ___ 2 ___ 3 ___ 4 ___ 5 ___ 6 ___ 7 ___ 8 ___ 9 ___ 10

Helped to change others' opinion of me - teachers/family

1 ___ 2 ___ 3 ___ 4 ___ 5 ___ 6 ___ 7 ___ 8 ___ 9 ___ 10

Helped me to work out a way forward and believe that I can succeed

1 ___ 2 ___ 3 ___ 4 ___ 5 ___ 6 ___ 7 ___ 8 ___ 9 ___ 10

Section 2 - Skills Learned

Tick the box if you agree with the statement.

I have learned to:

☐ Walk away physically

☐ Walk away mentally

☐ Ignore the problem / comment/ other person

☐ Use relaxation - deep breathing, counting etc.

☐ Use 'Stepped approaches' to solve problems

☐ Use a 'traffic light' method to solve a problem

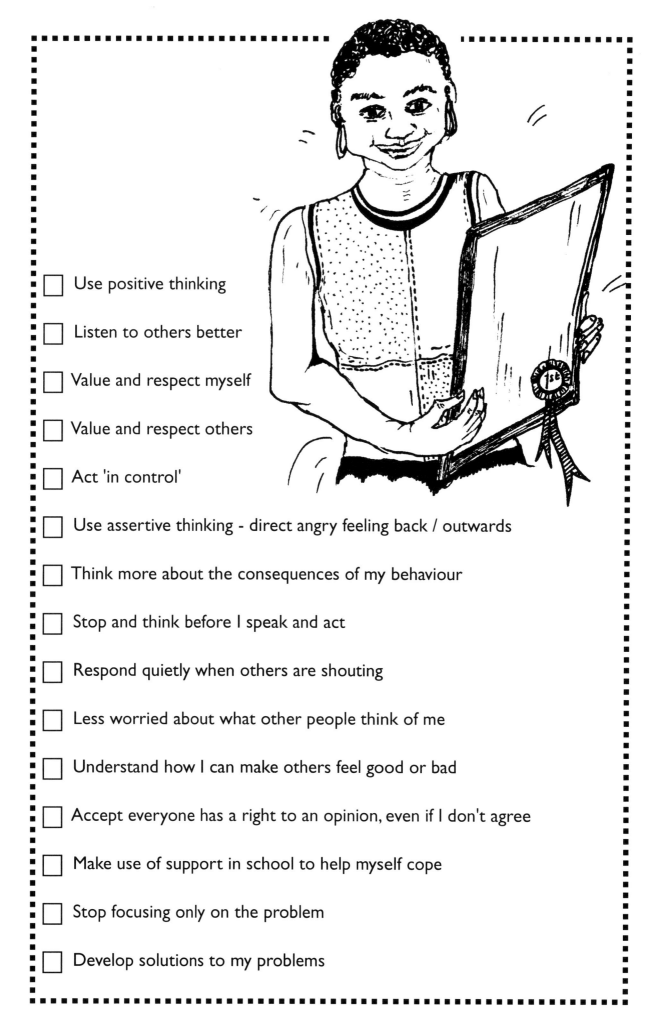

- [ ] Use positive thinking

- [ ] Listen to others better

- [ ] Value and respect myself

- [ ] Value and respect others

- [ ] Act 'in control'

- [ ] Use assertive thinking - direct angry feeling back / outwards

- [ ] Think more about the consequences of my behaviour

- [ ] Stop and think before I speak and act

- [ ] Respond quietly when others are shouting

- [ ] Less worried about what other people think of me

- [ ] Understand how I can make others feel good or bad

- [ ] Accept everyone has a right to an opinion, even if I don't agree

- [ ] Make use of support in school to help myself cope

- [ ] Stop focusing only on the problem

- [ ] Develop solutions to my problems

Section 3 - Identifying Changes

Did I meet my targets?   Yes / No

Say why

How did I change?

What changed around me?

Did others change to help me?

Section 4 - Planning Future Courses

How do you think we can improve this course?
Please give your suggestions and ideas.

What activities could we include in future courses?

What could we miss out?

What other skills could students learn?

**Thank you for your contribution You have completed the course
Well Done!**

Individual Action Plan

Name   **Date**

My progress so far:

Areas still to be improved:

⇒

⇒

⇒

My new targets:

⇒

⇒

⇒

⇒

Strategies and resources to achieve the new targets:

⇒

⇒

⇒

⇒

I will know if I have been successful if the following things happen:

⇒

⇒

⇒

⇒

I will evaluate the success

with _____

on _____

Follow on Work
and
Mentoring Form

FOLLOW ON WORK

In the introduction to this course it was clearly stated that students who had been involved in the crucial skills group would continue to need some form of support or provision after the course had finished. For some students it may be necessary to involve an outside agency in order to build on and further develop the work which has been initiated through these sessions. Such students will need to be identified via the usual school systems for working with students identified as having special educational needs.

However for all students involved in the course it is essential that a follow up meeting is organised in order to reflect on and evaluate progress and to identify any continuing needs. It is crucial that once students have been supported in this way that institutions continue to provide opportunities to ensure that students' needs continue to be met. As stated in the introduction this will call for a whole school approach to developing a listening time policy. Students readily respond to a miracle question but what we as educators should of course realise is that there are no miracle cures and affecting student behaviour is a long term commitment. Schools need to see that this kind of programme is merely a start in the development of a positive approach to ensuring the inclusion of students with emotional and behavioural difficulties. Staff need to accept and allow for the fact that students will respond differently to this kind of intervention and that some may require an opportunity to reinforce and revisit the learnt skills if or when things go wrong for them. To ignore such students would be counter-productive. Any success needs to be built on and be celebrated. Even when things go wrong it will always be possible to re-establish and maintain the positive, solution focused approach.

In the follow up meeting students can review action plans and again make use of the scaling activity. New targets can be set and incorporated into IEPs. This meeting can also provide an opportunity to share and celebrate successes and confirm positive relationships.

The content of the meeting will prompt staff to review appropriate interventions for inclusion, such as PSHE, media and arts' curriculum and look for opportunities to celebrate achievement within this framework.

The Mentoring Scheme

At the start of this course it was suggested that schools may wish to implement a mentoring scheme to run alongside the crucial skills course. Such a system would allow students to work consistently with a significant adult in the school context with whom they could build a trusting and positive relationship. It would also would allow for the regular setting of appropriate, achievable targets and encourage the students to become more reflective and develop greater self-awareness.

A suggested format for recording a weekly mentoring session is included. This form initially asks the student to make use of the scaling activity as detailed in the student interview/session one. Students who rate themselves at zero feel extremely negative about the week. A rating of five would imply that they felt OK but recognised the need to make further improvements and ten would indicate that the student had experienced a perfect week!

Secondly the student should reflect back on the previous week identifying both positives and negatives. This further develops the solution focused approach in that the student is asked not only to identify any problems and how they dealt with them but also to suggest what they could have done differently, i.e. what would be a more positive response next time?

The form requires both the student and the mentor to agree whether or not targets have been achieved and to record the type of support currently on offer to the student, e.g. time out facility, use of homework club, alternative counselling provision, etc.

The weekly record requires the student and mentor to agree and record targets for the coming week and to identify the date and time of the next meeting. Students need to specify the rating that they would then like to achieve during the coming week. Naturally every aspect of this process is crucial but perhaps the most vital part of the whole process is for mentors to provide positive feedback and recognise the student's progress in the weekly feedback call to parents/carers. This could also provide an opportunity for staff and parents/carers to ensure a consistent approach and programme for the student which significantly links the two of the most important aspects of the student's life at school and home.

Mentoring Scheme

Name
Tutor Group   **Date of Meeting**

Pupil Weekly Rating   /10

Pupil's Views
How has this week been (good things and bad things)
Did you have any difficulties? How were they dealt with? Could <u>you</u> have done anything differently?

Reviewing Targets - Pupil and Mentor comments
Have targets been achieved? What support has been offered?

Targets for the coming week: Pupil and Mentor to agree:

*

*

*

*

Next meeting   **date**   **time**
Next week I would like to achieve a score of   /10

Weekly feedback call to parents/carers

Date/time of next call

96

References

Excellence for All Children: Meeting SEN. (1997) London. DfEE.

Furman, B. and Ahola, T. (1992) Solution Talk: Hosting Therapeutic Conversations. New York. Norton

George, E., Iveson, C. & Rather, H. (1990) Problem to Solution: Brief Therapy with Individuals and Families. London. Brief Therapy Publication.

Lethem, J. (1994) Moved to Tears, Moved to Action: solution focused brief therapy with women and children. London. Brief Therapy Publication.

Rhodes, J. & Ajmal, Y. (1995) Solution Focused Thinking in Schools. London. Brief Therapy Publication.

Social Inclusion : Pupil Support. (1999) London. DfEE.

The Code of Practice on the Identification and Assessment of Special Educational Needs. (1994) London. DFE.

Times Educational Supplement. November 13, 1998. Hinds, J. TES Update-School Management. London. Times Supplements Limited.

de Shazer, S. (1988) Clues : Investigating Solutions in Brief Therapy. New York. Norton.

Don't forget to visit our website for all our latest publications, news and reviews.

www.luckyduck.co.uk

New publications every year on our specialist topics:

- **Emotional Literacy**

- **Self-esteem**

- **Bullying**

- **Positive Behaviour Management**

- **Circle Time**

- **Anger Management**

- **Asperger's Syndrome**

- **Eating Disorders**

3 Thorndale Mews, Clifton, Bristol, BS8 2HX | Tel: +44 (0) 117 973 2881 Fax: +44 (0) 117 973 1707